THE EAST INDIA COMPANY
BOOK OF
TEA

ANTONY WILD

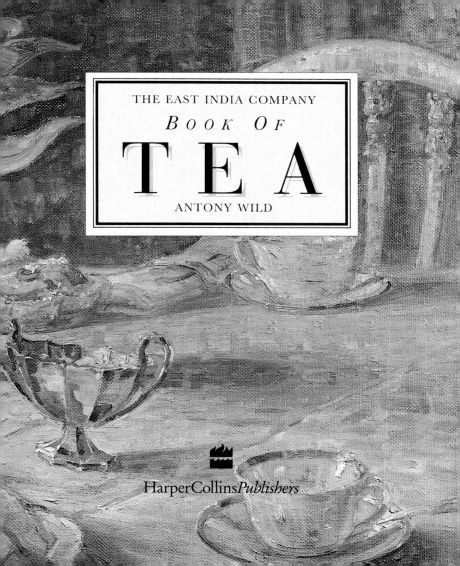

THE EAST INDIA COMPANY

BOOK OF

TEA

ANTONY WILD

HarperCollins*Publishers*

First published in 1994 by
HarperCollins*Publishers,* London

Text © Antony Victor Wild

Antony Wild asserts the moral right to
be identified as the author of this work

Commissioning Editor: Polly Powell
Editor: Lisa Eaton
Cover Design: Ian Butterworth
Designer: Rachel Smyth
Picture Researcher: Nadine Bazar

The publishers and author would like to thank
David Hutton, Drew Smith, Valerie Light, Robert Baldwin,
Edward Bramah, and the Tea Council.

**A catalogue record for this book is
available from the British Library**

ISBN 0 00 412 738 2

Colour reproduction by Colourscan, Singapore
Printed and bound in Italy

Contents

The Armorial Bearings of the Company of Merchants of London
trading into the East Indies granted by Garter and Clarenceux
Kings of Arms in 1600, and as borne and used until 1709

*F*ounded by the Royal Charter of Queen Elizabeth I in 1600, the East India Company was the single most powerful economic force that the world has ever seen. Its influence reached out to all continents, and the consequences of its actions, both great and small, are the very fabric of history. The Company created British India; founded Hong Kong and Singapore; caused the Boston Tea Party; employed Captain Kidd to combat piracy; held Napoleon captive; and made the fortune of Elihu Yale who founded his famous university with the proceeds.

The Stars and Stripes was inspired by its flag, its shipyards provided the model for St Petersburg, its London chapel set the pattern for New England churches, its administration still forms the basis of Indian bureaucracy, and its corporate structure was the earliest example of a joint stock company. It introduced tea to Britain and India, woollens to Japan, chintzes to America, spices to the West Indies, opium to China, porcelain to Russia, and polo to Persia. It had its own armies, navies, currencies, and territories as diverse as the tiny Spice Island, Pulo Run – later exchanged for Manhattan

– and the 'Jewel in the Crown', India itself. As *The Times* newspaper reported in 1874 when the Company was finally absorbed by the Crown: 'It is just as well to record that it accomplished a work such as in the whole history of the human race no other Company ever attempted and, as such, is ever likely to attempt in the years to come.'

East India House

The Story of Tea

Origins

*T*here are many legends about the discovery of tea, none of which has any solid foundation in historical fact. But the world requires an explanation for the discovery of one of its most popular drinks, and the ancient Chinese story of the Emperor Wan Tu is by far the best.

A Chinese family being served with tea, 19th century

Wan Tu and the Discovery of Tea

The Emperor of China, Wan Tu, an evil, cruel and despotic man, was overthrown by his first minister and banished to a remote southern part of China. He sat in the shade of a large bush plotting his revenge. Driven by poverty to drinking only hot water, he was delighted one day when some of the leaves of the bush fell into his saucepan of boiling water, and he discovered that the resulting brew was tasty, refreshing and relaxing. It cleared his mind so effectively that he sat under the bush for seven years drinking it, learning to regret his former tyrannies and vowing to make amends. He named the drink Tai, *meaning peace, in recognition of its effect on him. He returned to the capital city in disguise and became a valued adviser to his former first minister. He was so wise and so beloved by the people that when the minister died he was chosen as his successor, and ruled justly for many years, introducing tea to the nation. Only on his deathbed did Wan Tu reveal his true identity, and to honour the wonderful changes that tea had wrought in him, the poet Lu Yu wrote the* Tai Ching, *the famous book of tea.*

There is no doubt that tea was used in ancient China for many thousands of years, and more than likely in Burma (now Myanmar) and Siam (Thailand) as well. At first it was used for medicinal purposes, but later as a beverage. The Japanese learnt the art of tea cultivation and drinking from their neighbour in the 12th century, and the fine pottery and porcelain produced in these countries for tea drinking suggests that it was an important part of their lives. Russia was the first Western nation to import tea, on camel trains across the Gobi desert. The tea was compressed into bricks, and the round trip from China took three years.

The tea trade

The East India Company had a monopoly on all trade to Britain from the East and, although it was originally set up to trade in spices, the Company quickly found that there were many other products from the Orient, such as tea, that could find a ready market back home.

Tea drinking had been fashionable with the Portuguese since they had established their trading post at Macao on the Chinese coast in the 16th century. When Charles II of England married the Portuguese princess Catherine of Braganza, she introduced the English Court to the pleasures of tea drinking and within a short time it was hugely popular. The first use of the word in the English language is contained in a letter written in 1615 by a Company officer in Japan to a colleague – and the Company, which had long been aware of the existence of tea, quickly realized that there was money to be made from this new fashion. By the end of the 18th century the Company was making more money from the trade in tea than from anything else, and a fleet of beautiful sailing ships called 'EastIndiamen' was plying the oceans between Europe and Canton.

Catherine of Braganza

The Boston Tea Party

One of the central events in the quest of the American Colonies for independence from the British stemmed from the East India Company's need for a solution to a financial crisis.

Tea had been very popular on the north-eastern coast of America since the 1650s – most of it smuggled. Meanwhile, not only was the East India Company in debt, it had also built up substantial stocks of tea in London. The Company persuaded the British government to pass the Tea Act of 1773 to allow them to send tea to America and to sell it there at a price that included high British duties. The ships with the first consignment berthed at Griffin's Wharf, Boston, where, as a sign of protest against the British, the tea chests were unceremoniously tipped into the sea by patriots dressed as native Americans – an event which came to be known as the Boston Tea Party. The same happened with later shipments to Charleston, Philadelphia, New York and Annapolis, but it is the Boston Tea Party that has lived on in American folklore. However, contrary to legend, the former colony did not give up tea altogether, and the East India Company was back in business selling tea to America by the early 1800s.

Tea trade in China, early 19th century

The East India Company was not happy that the monopoly of supplies for this vital trade lay in the hands of the Chinese, and by the 1840s the Company had established its own plantations in Assam and Darjeeling, north India. The new large-scale estates were copied in other colonies like Ceylon (now Sri Lanka) and Kenya. The tea produced from these plantations was the fermented black tea commonly drunk today, rather than the predominantly unfermented green tea produced by the cottage tea industry in China.

Dr Johnson described himself as 'a hardened and shameless tea drinker.'

Tea today

Tea is one of the world's most popular beverages. The Irish are the world's biggest consumers, drinking on average eight cups a day per person, whilst the biggest consuming nation is India, where *chai* is an essential part of daily life. It is estimated that by the year 2,000 India will consume more tea than it produces – and it is the world's biggest producer! Some of the finest teas now come from East Africa, where it was introduced only this century. The world's best-selling brands are Liptons and Brooke Bond. The world's most expensive tea is a Makaibari F.T.G.F.O.P., or Flowery Tippy Golden Flowery Orange Pekoe, bought in 1992 for £240 ($360) per kilogramme.

Gladstone, the British Prime Minister under Queen Victoria, used to fill his hot water bottle with tea, not so he could take a nip in the night, but because he wanted to be soothed by his favourite drink.

How Tea is Produced

The tea bush

*T*he tea bush, *Camellia sinensis,* looks very similar to the bush used for the common privet hedge, *Ligustrum ovalifolium.* A wild tea bush left to its own devices can grow to a height of 50 ft (15 m), but this is impractical for tea pickers. On all estates, whether large or small, the tea bush is kept to a height of about 4 ft (1.2 m). During the growing season, which varies according to altitude, climate and latitude, the tea bush may need picking once every few days to ensure that only the best tips – the young tender leaves – are plucked. As a result the tea industry is very labour intensive and provides a considerable source of employment in many of the Third World countries where it is grown. Only in parts of Russia has the tea-picking process been mechanized, but the tea produced is very coarse and of a poor quality.

Green tea

As with tea drinking, the ancient tradition of tea cultivation is still alive in China today. Green tea, which forms a relatively small proportion of the amount of tea that China now produces, is grown, plucked, sorted and manufactured

Processing tea in China, c. 1840

using many of the same techniques that were practised 2,000 years ago. It is very much a peasant industry orientated around village life, with a central factory providing the main focus of the processing of the tea leaves.

For many hundreds of years China remained the principal source of tea for the world, and still today the warm, fertile, semitropical climate in the high hills provides the ideal growing conditions for the tea bush. Grown on even terraces on the well-drained plantations, the tea bush matures after four or five years, producing two leaves and a bud, which

Cultivating the tea bushes

together make the tea leaf. The sorting and grading of the leaves is still carried out by hand, and the freshly picked green leaves are dried in a pan resembling a wok. As the moisture is driven off, the leaves are then gently rolled into curls which eventually form the green tea.

Samuel Pepys noted in his diary in 1666, 'I did send for a cup of tea, a China drink of which I never drunk before.'

Recipe for Gilgit Tea
Add a few pods of cardamom to a pot of Chinese green tea. Allow to brew for five minutes.

Lapsang Souchong

Japan Pilo Chun

A selection of teas from around the world

China Gui Hua

Kenya High Mountain

China 'Emperor' Keemun

Gunpowder Green

Choicest Fancy Formosa Oolong

*Mountains of the Moon
from Rwanda*

Special Estate Tippy Assam

Earl Grey

*Special Estate Darjeeling
(Badamtam Estate)*

Ceylon Orange Pekoe

Black tea

Modern tea production is based on the large estate system pioneered in India. The tea bushes on the plantation are all kept to a level growth to make picking easier. Two leaves and a bud only are picked, and the pickers are paid by the weight of tea. The quality of the tea that they pick is checked, then the fresh green leaves need to be dried. This first process, known as 'withering', is carried out in large troughs.

In order to manufacture black tea, which is commonly used in tea bags and represents over 95 per cent of the world's production today, the tea leaves have to be 'cut', 'torn' and 'curled' – hence the name C.T.C. tea. This is where the 'withered' leaf is broken down into smaller particles, which is done on a large scale using machinery. In the 'tearing' process the cells of the tea are exposed and the oxidation process begins. The more the tea is 'cut' and 'torn', the more the green turns to brown. By this stage the tea is quite dry, most of the moisture having been driven off during the machining and drying processes. Eventually, once the manufacturing process is finished, the tea is ready to be put into chests which are then shipped all over the world. Before the invention of tea bags, black teas used to be produced by the orthodox process, which breaks down the leaves into relatively larger particles, resulting in a slower-brewing tea. The best known of these are the whole leaf and large broken leaf grades of Orange Pekoe and Broken Orange Pekoe.

Unloading tea at the docks, 1877

Oolong, Lapsang Souchong and Gunpowder

Oolong teas are semi-fermented – that is, they are roughly halfway between a green tea and a black tea. Originally they were cultivated in south China and were exported in large quantities. These types gave rise to the modern black teas. The best examples today come from Formosa (now Taiwan), and are renowned for their peachy flavour.

Lapsang Souchong was all the rage in the 1870s, and was raced back to Britain and America on the *Cutty Sark* and the *Flying Cloud*. It has a dark, thick 'liquor' and a pronounced smoky flavour. There are many stories concerning how it acquires this flavour; being kept in a confined space with burning bamboo or burning roots seems to be the favoured explanation, but the most romantic is that it is exposed to the smoke from a lighted rope dipped in tar. Most experts agree that the prewar Lapsangs were cured in the smoke from white pine wood.

Gunpowder tea is a green tea whose leaves are rolled into little tight balls resembling cartridge shot. The tea keeps better than conventional green teas; the leaves unfurl when the tea is brewed.

John Wesley noted in himself a 'paralytick disorder', and with great difficulty gave up drinking tea and urged his followers to do likewise after observing that all he saw in London appeared to be suffering from the same thing, 'nerves all unstrung, bodily strength decayed.'

Strange Names and Curious Teas

*The teas exported from China to Europe and America in the 17th
and 18th centuries were predominantly green teas, and were
called by curious names, most now sadly disappeared, such as
Young Hyson, Bing, Caper, and Twankay (after which Gilbert
and Sullivan's* Widow
Twankey *was named).
However, no tea was
stranger than that
reserved for the
Emperor and his court,
which came from wild tea
bushes in Yunnan province.
These grew to such a height
that it was impossible for the
tips to be plucked except
by specially trained
monkeys. About
200 pounds of
Imperial
Monkey-Picked
Tea were
produced
each
season.*

Ship to shore

Tea has long been associated with the romance of the Tea Clippers, the beautiful sailing vessels of the late 19th century which were later replaced by steamships. However, the fashion for tea in Europe and America gave impetus to the rise of a new class of sailing vessel from the earliest days of the trade. To service the demand for goods from the East, the East India Company developed a fleet of high-capacity sailing ships known as 'EastIndiamen', which were fast, sleek

EastIndiamen in the China Seas, by William Huggins

and well armed, and had well-trained and highly disciplined crews. These served until well into the 19th century, by which time the tea trade had become so important that other nations, particularly America, had evolved their own ships to accommodate it. The 'Baltimore Clipper' type proved too small, but eventually the Americans became so adept at

Modern tea chests

shipbuilding that their Tea Clipper 'Lightning' became the fastest of them all, once covering 436 miles in 24 hours.

Initially tea was shipped from China in porcelain jars and pots (at that time regarded as far less valuable than the tea they contained), which provided clean and watertight storage. As the trade grew, and as the value of porcelain in its own right came to be appreciated, wooden tea chests were introduced which were also easier to store on ships. These were initially very large – the chests thrown into Boston harbour weighed as much as 450 pounds – but they were steadily reduced in size as time went on. The tea chests used today weigh about 100 pounds.

Nowadays the shipping of tea has none of the romance of former years; the chests are stacked in containers which sit aboard ungainly container ships for the voyage to their destination. The famous tea warehouses which used to line the river banks have been replaced by huge warehouses sited by convenient motorways.

A question of taste

The tea auction in London is still the largest tea auction in the world. A large sample of the tea is drawn by a broker, and this is split up and sent to individual traders who buy the teas for the major brands. The teas are prepared for tasting, and boiling water is poured onto a measured portion of the tea. It is allowed to brew for five minutes, poured out into the tasting bowls, and allowed to cool. It is then ready for tasting.

Tea tasting terms: Appearance

Tippy – indicates the presence of the golden or silver coloured leaves from the tip of the budding tea leaf
Wiry – when a leaf is tightly twisted it resembles a piece of wire. This will open out when the tea is brewed
Stalky – the reddish stalk of the tea leaf may look unappealing, but can yield a respectable 'liquor'
Bright – after infusion the leaf has a good, pronounced colour, usually orange or coppery
Dull – after infusion the leaf appears dark brown or green, likely to produce an inferior liquor

Tea tasting at auction, 1897

*The poet Percy Bysshe Shelley wrote:
'The liquid doctors rail at, and that I
will quaff in spite of them, and when I die
we'll toss up which died first of drinking tea.'*

Tea tasting terms: Liquor

Liquor – refers to the liquid produced after the leaves have been infused – in other words, the tea that we drink

Body – the sensation of the weight of the liquor on the palate

Coarse – the harsh, vegetable flavour of low-quality teas

Plain – lacking in desirable characteristics

Point – a pronounced favourable sharpness of flavour

Soft – a rather dull, flat character

Sweaty – a highly undesirable fruity, sour flavour

Bright – a lively, refreshing flavour

Malty – a favourable characteristic, often appearing in Assam tea

The tea leaves are spread out on the lid of the pot; this enables the tea buyer to examine the colour and size of the infusion, which can make a difference to their assessment of the tea's quality. The auction catalogue provides information on the estate where each of the teas came from and their lot number. Each tea is then assessed and given a value. At the auctions these lots of tea are then sold to the highest bidder. Quite often a buyer may not want all the chests of a particular lot and will then split it with another buyer.

Once the buyer has bought a tea, he or she then has to decide what role it is going to play in the blends. Tea blends may contain up to 30 different teas mostly bought at the London auction. A blend is basically a recipe, and the skill of

Afternoon tea was invented by Anna, Duchess of Bedford, to fill the gap between lunch and supper.

the blender ensures that the tea tastes the same as the previous recipe, even though the new blend may incorporate teas from completely different estates and even countries. The blend is then sent up to the tea factory ready to be packed and sold. The required chests of tea are assembled and then emptied into a machine which rotates the tea and mixes the different lots together. Up to several tons of tea can be mixed together at any one time in the machines.

Some blends are for so-called 'loose' tea, which goes directly into packets lined with foil or paper. These are still popular with connoisseurs who maintain that the quality of the tea brewed in this way is better than that from the tea bag. Speciality teas are thus often sold in this form. However most tea around the world these days is sold in tea bags, and these are packed on special fast-moving tea bag machines.

Rudyard Kipling wrote, 'To lack tea for a week is to knock the bottom out of the Universe.'

Recipe for Tea Cocktail

Mix 1 ½ fl oz (45ml) of gin with 1 ½ fl oz (45ml) of strong tea. Add a dash of Angostura bitters and a dash of pure vanilla essence. Let it cool, then pour into a glass with ice cubes, adding lemonade to taste.

Varieties of Tea

Where tea comes from

*T*ea is grown mainly in tropical countries around the world, but is actively cultivated as far north as Russia and as far south as Argentina. Because the picking is very labour intensive, it is grown where wages are low to keep costs down. There is one tea brand in the United States made from tea from an American estate, but it is small scale and highly priced.

Tea bushes can be grown at all altitudes, but a basic rule is that the higher they grow, the better the tea they produce. They can survive some frost, but are happiest at altitude in tropical or semitropical regions where temperatures do not vary too much, and where there is plenty of moisture. The reason why altitude is important to the eventual quality of the tea is simple; the cooler air restricts the speed of growth of the plant, producing a more tender leaf with a fuller flavour. At low altitude the bush grows profusely, resulting in a coarser flavour.

Region by region

India

From the middle of the 19th century Darjeeling became known for producing some of the world's finest tea. Some of today's estates are situated over 7,000 ft (2,134 m) up. The best **Darjeeling** is tea which is light in colour and delicate of

From 'A Glimpse of Assam'

Recipe for Planters' Sorbet

Allow ¾ oz (20g) of good quality Darjeeling tea to stand for five minutes in ½ pint (300ml) of freshly drawn, boiling water. Sieve the extract through a muslin bag, and then melt 6 oz (175g) of candied sugar into the hot tea. Add the juice of two lemons after it has cooled, then freeze as fast as possible. When it is half frozen, carefully mix in half the white of an egg, and allow to freeze completely. The sorbet should be soft when served in pre-cooled glasses which have had their rims dipped in crème de menthe and sugar.

flavour, with a noticeable 'point' or astringency. The teas produced at the beginning of the season, known as the 'first flush', are noted for their exquisite delicacy, and the later 'second flush' teas are the most prized of all.

The first 12 chests of **Assam** tea were delivered for auction in

Tea plantations in Darjeeling and Assam, India

1838. The area now produces great quantities of tea which at their best produce a full, reddish 'liquor' and have a rich, deep flavour. They are versatile teas which perform well in all water types, and are frequently used in stronger Breakfast blends.

The Dooars region, between Darjeeling and Assam produces good blending teas, as do the Nilgiri and Kerela regions of south India.

China

Lapsang Souchong has a distinctive smoky flavour – the 'kipper of teas'. **Keemun** has a light, flowery, sweet flavour with an orchid aroma. **Yunnan** teas from the southern part of the country have something of the character of Assam teas as well as a characteristic Chinese flavour, and **Gunpowder** is a green tea with a subtle, fresh flavour. China also produces large quantities of fairly good black tea which finds its way into many blends, and provides a useful base for flavoured teas.

Ceylon

Tea plants were first established in Ceylon in 1839 at the

Botanical Gardens in Peradeniya, and the first tea estate was planted in 1840. Although they vary from region to region, good Ceylon teas grown at high altitude typically produce a golden 'liquor' and a fine aromatic flavour. The two principal growing areas are the eastern province of Uva, which produces teas with a fuller body and more pungent flavour, and Dimbula in the west of the island, producing tea with a finer, softer flavour. Other notable Ceylon teas come from Kandy and Nuwara Eliya.

East Africa

East Africa produces some of the world's finest teas, generally with a bright, orangey 'liquor' and a brisk refreshing taste.

Kenya now supplies more tea to the British market than either India or Ceylon, as their quick-brewing, bright coloured teas are ideal for tea bags. The first tea grown outside Asia was cultivated in East Africa in 1878, and Malawi now has a highly organized industry, producing teas of a good average quality. Rwanda reigns supreme amongst the East African teas: top-quality Rwanda teas are equal to the world's best with their pronounced orange colour and bright flavour.

Other countries

Teas from the other main producing countries, whilst exported in large quantities, are rarely of a sufficiently high quality to be drunk on their own and need to be blended. Indonesia, Tanzania, Bangladesh, Argentina and Russia all produce teas of this sort.

Speciality and blended teas

There is no inherent difference between the teas used in so-called speciality teas and those used in blending, other than that speciality teas tend to be named after a defined region, and are usually of a superior quality. English Breakfast is considered a speciality tea, but in reality is no more than a high-quality blended tea which contains teas of several different origins. At the top end of the market it is possible to buy a single grade of tea called a 'self-drinker' from a single estate, but even most speciality tea brands will contain teas from a particular region blended together.

Reading the leaves

Whilst in the West reading the tea leaves is a fairly recent and much derided method of fortune-telling, it has long been taken seriously in the East. Eastern scholars are quick to point out that the ceremonial uses of tea drinking as an aid to meditation in China and Japan imply that the ancients believed that the configuration of tea leaves in the cup after drinking reflected the state of the world at that particular moment. Students of the I Ching, *an ancient Chinese book of wisdom, will be familiar with the principle.*

Professional 'tasseographers', as the tea-leaf readers like to be known, work by swirling the tea around in a shallow teacup anti-clockwise three times, then placing

Reading the tea leaves, late 19th century

it upside down in a saucer to drain the liquid. Three more anticlockwise turns finish with the handle pointing towards the enquirer, and the cup is then turned the right way up and scrutinized. The tea leaves then fall into various patterns which are ascribed certain properties according to where they are in the cup. For example, a pattern of leaves in the shape of a knife in the 'home' portion of the cup near the handle suggests divorce. At the far side it suggests treachery at work. Some of the interpretations are fairly obvious – a ball, for instance, suggests the ability to bounce back from problems – whilst others are downright obscure – a chestnut tree suggests justice. Although tasseography handbooks show tea leaves forming themselves easily into such complex shapes as a knapsack or a clergyman, in reality it is not so easy to see any particular shape. The advent of the tea bag, however, would seem to foretell the doom of this particular branch of fortune-telling.

Flavoured and Scented Teas

The story of Earl Grey

Many tea companies say that they use the 'original' Earl Grey recipe, which they claim was given to the second Earl Grey whilst on a mission to China. In reality however, the Earl never went to China. So how did the recipe come about ?

Earl Grey is tea scented with bergamot. The use of flavourings with tea was actually first observed by Sir George Staunton in China in 1793. He noted particularly the use of orange flavouring. The Chinese bitter orange, *Citrus aurantium*, had been known in Europe since the times of

George Thomas Staunton with his mother, Lady Anne Staunton

Marco Polo, and was grown in Seville and Sicily. Its oil, neroli, was valued in the perfume industry. However the *Citrus aurantium* grown on the Italian mainland around Bergamo in Calabria gradually changed to form *Citrus aurantium* subspecies *bergamot*, with quite distinct flavour characteristics (*see illustration on page 43*). The oil extract from the bergamot plant became popular in the 18th and 19th centuries as a flavouring for snuff and gin, and later, as we know, for tea. As bergamot was a subspecies peculiar to Bergamo, it is clear that the Earl Grey recipe cannot have originated in China as claimed.

On his return from China, Staunton reported his observations of the use of orange flavouring to Sir Joseph Banks, an inveterate experimenter with exotic foods since his days sailing with Captain Cook. Banks had a teahouse in the basement of his house in Soho Square, London, and may well have experimented with various tea flavourings along the lines suggested by Staunton. Inevitably the bergamot, as a close relation of the Chinese bitter orange, was tried, and the recipe for Earl Grey was thus invented.

The most likely explanation of Earl Grey's link to the tea lies in the fact that at the time when the tea was coming to public attention he was an extremely popular reforming prime minister, particularly with the newly enfranchised and wealthy urban bourgeoisie. Although he was an acquaintance of Banks, and may well have enjoyed his concoction, there is no record of the Earl adopting it as a particular favourite, and it is more likely that the blend was named after him because of his political popularity.

Recipe for Flaming Spiced Tea

Take a pot of tea brewed to normal strength and pour into suitable glasses. Crush a few cloves and some cinammon, and place in a heat-resistant dish, then pour in rum. Set light to it, and pour a little of the resulting mixture into each glass. Sweeten to taste.

Scents and spices

The Chinese regularly scented and flavoured their teas.
Particular favourites were the teas flavoured with jasmine
blossoms, orange blossoms, cherry blossoms, rose petals and
even cowslips. Jasmine blossom tea is still widely produced in
China. The use of spices, however, dates from the start of
European interest in tea. Both the Dutch and the English
were initially very keen to trade in spices, and after tea
became fashionable it was inevitable that they combined the
two. The Arab world is particularly keen on the use of
cardomom with tea, and cinnamon seems to have been used
since the earliest days.

'Chow Chow' man, a street tea seller in Macao

Cinnamon and The Royal Tea

Charles II of England established a menagerie of rare and exotic animals and birds in Birdcage Walk, St James Park. He expected the East India Company to present him with new specimens each time a ship returned from the East. When, in 1664, a returning captain reported to the Court of Directors of the East India Company that their agents in the East Indies had failed to make provision for the King, they scoured the ship for a suitable gift, and the minute book records: 'The Governour acquainting ye Court that ye Factors haveing in every place failed ye company of such things as they writt for to have presented his majesty with and that his majesty might not find himself wholly neglected by ye company, he was of the opinion if ye Court thinck fitt that a silver case of oile of cinnamon and some good tea, be provided for that end.' It is known that this was the first time that the King had received tea from the Company, and it is tempting to think that he may have ordered it to be combined with the 'oile of cinnamon' to make one of the first spiced teas. It is certainly no coincidence that within weeks of this gift being made to the King, the import of tea began in earnest.

Best of the Brews

Brewing up

*T*he best 'cuppa' (cup of tea) is made in a pot which has been thoroughly warmed beforehand. Add one heaped teaspoon of tea leaves per person and one for the pot, (or the equivalent in tea bags), then add **boiling** water. The most common complaint is that the water is not hot enough to make a decent 'cuppa'. The water should be freshly drawn from the tap or bottle. Allow five minutes for the tea to brew.

Left: Afternoon Tea, after Kate Greenaway

Naming the Brew

The British are so keen on brewing tea properly that they have different words for the verb 'to brew' in different regions: 'mash' in northern England, 'mask' in Scotland, 'soak' in Cornwall and 'wet' in south-western dialect.

Each to their own

Tibetans boil brick tea from China with soda and salt, and then churn it into rancid yak's butter to form a thick oily liquid.

Paraguay or Jesuit's Tea is not tea at all. It is maté, the infusion of a leaf of a bush rather like a holly tree. It produces a slightly bitter flavour.

Russians brew their tea in a samovar, in which water is kept hot by a charcoal cylinder. The brew is kept going for most of the day, and full teapots are drawn off at will. A spoonful of jam is added as a sweetener.

Scandinavian afternoon tea, late 19th century

Japan produces some fine green teas, including Sencha, a steamed tea grown from unshaded bushes, developed in the 18th century. Sencha is almost undrinkable to the Western palate, having a pronounced astringency, due to its high ascorbic acid content. Matsucha, the teas used for the tea ceremony, come from shaded bushes, and the dried leaves are stone-milled to produce a fine, fluffy powder.

Japanese tea ceremony

Recipe for Moroccan Mint Tea

Pour standard strength black tea into glasses containing sprigs of fresh mint. Allow some time for the tea to absorb the flavour. Sweeten to taste. In Arab countries the tea is drunk whilst the mint is still in the glass.

Indians frequently brew their tea by adding it to boiling buffalo milk, then adding a few favourite spices such as cardamom or cloves. It is served in small cups, sweetened.

Jonathan Swift claimed, 'Tea is water bewitched!'

In America iced tea is far more popular. The simplest way to produce a good iced tea is to brew a pot of tea to double the normal strength (2 heaped teaspoons per person) and, while it is hot, pour it into glasses full of crushed ice or ice cubes. Adding some mint to the tea gives a distinct flavour.

Late 18th century tea garden

Britain

Tea drinking is often considered a quintessentially British activity, but, in fact, coffee was much more fashionable during the 17th century, and it was only when the Court, under the influence of Catherine of Braganza, started to drink tea that it became fashionable. Covered tea gardens, where people could wander around, talk and drink tea, sprang up in London, such as those at Vauxhall and Ranelagh.

Tea caddies

As tea was so expensive in the 18th century, it was considered essential for the mistress of the house to be able to keep it under lock and key lest the servants found the temptation too much. As a result, the tea caddy evolved, a small box often fitted with a lock and key. It kept the tea safe at the same time as being a fine decorative ornament. Like other tea-making paraphernalia, the tea caddy moved from being simply a convenient safe storage container to becoming a valued and valuable part of the tea-drinking ritual.

18th century French tea ceremony, with caddy

Teapots

In the 18th century traders found that Chinese Yi-Hsing red earthenware teapots were also useful as ballast for their tea cargoes, and these were the antecedents of the 'Brown Betty' teapot. Until the 1760s and the meteoric rise of Josiah Wedgwood, there were no teapots made in Europe and America other than those made of silver. Thereafter the demand for tea and tea accessories became so strong that an industry grew up to supply the need – teapots, tea-infusers, sugar bowls and spoons, strainers – all became necessities for the tea-drinking ritual. Wedgwood started making pots from a creamy earthenware known as 'Queen's Ware' because it was liked by Queen Charlotte, but later became best known for his stoneware designs. He always asked his wife to test new teapot shapes, and was never more pleased than when 'Mrs Wedgwood has tried our new teapots … and gives them her sanction, as the best and pleasantest in the hand that she has ever used.' In time the treasured teapot became the excuse for extravagant designs by manufacturers, commemorating events, caricaturing politicians and honouring sovereigns.

Teapots: porcelain early 18th century Meissen; silver Queen Anne teapot and stand; pottery Mickey Mouse novelty

Tea came to be seen as a valuable commodity and at one stage in the 18th century tea taxes constituted over 10 per cent of the entire revenue from taxation of the country. As a result tea smuggling became commonplace, and adulteration with nettle leaves and other plants of the hedgerow was commonly complained about. With a pound of tea costing a working man's monthly wages, it is surprising to find that it was so popular at every level of society. With the development of tea estates in India and Ceylon, so the price came down and it was possible for the whole nation to enjoy good freshly brewed tea on a daily basis.

Afternoon tea, early 20th century

France

The Compagnie des Indes was set up as a rival to the East India Company of England and it established trading posts such as Pondicherry in southern India. Tea was used for a while as a herbal medicine, as Louis XIV was told that in China and Japan no-one suffered from gout, apoplexy or epilepsy because of tea. In the end even that interest dwindled, and the French maintained that the British only resorted to drinking tea because they had no wine. Today tea drinking is seen as a quintessentially British activity and is treated as very much a gourmet activity by a small number of devotees.

The fashion for tea in France, 1893

The United States

In America tea had been fashionable on the north-eastern coast since the 1650s – in fact, it is probable that it was a well-established favourite with the Dutch burghers of New Amsterdam before it became widely known in England. Tea gardens modelled on those of London flourished on Manhattan, and by the 1760s America was importing over a million pounds of tea a year.

Holland

The Dutch had established trading links with Japan by 1610, and brought tea back to Holland from there. It was given as a gift by the Dutch East India Company (V.O.C.) to the Court, and set the fashion there long before it reached England. Again, the medicinal qualities of tea rather than its taste appealed and it was sold by chemists. Although it never really caught on in Holland, the V.O.C. trade in tea flourished, much of it smuggled into England and America.

Germany

Through Dutch influence the Germans discovered tea, but it only became popular in the northern district of Ostfriesland and around Bremen. It remains so today, with some of the highest prices for 'first flush' Darjeeling teas being paid by tea merchants from these areas.

Index

Picture Credits

The publisher thanks the photographers and organisations for their kind
permission to reproduce the following photographs in this book:

Boston Harbour from Constitution Wharf, (detail), by Robert Salmon
US Naval Academy, Annapolis, Maryland/Bridgeman Art Library,
jacket photograph;

Royal Doulton 1;
Christie's Images 2–3, 46, 57 (top and middle);
Mary Evans Picture Library 5, 7, 8 (top), 17, 34 (top), 37, 49, 52, 54, 63, 64;
Hong Kong Shanghai Bank 8, 44;
Edward Bramah Tea and Coffee Museum 11, 19, 57 (bottom);
N Currier, 1846/Museum of the City of New York 56.300.821
(The Harry T Peters Collection) 12–13;
Bridgeman Art Library 14;
The Advertising Archives 15, 31, 53;
Ann Ronan/Image Select 16, 48–9;
Jean-Loup Charmet 18, 26, 39, 50, 60–61;
Theo Bergström 20–21
The Robert Opie Collection 23, 32, 34;
Hulton Deutsch 24;
National Maritime Museum 27;
Christian Sarramon 28;
Museum of London 30;
Eileen Tweedy/courtesy The Linnean Society 35, 43;
Francesco Venturi 36;
York City Art Gallery/Bridgeman Art Library 40–41;
Whitford & Hughes, London/Bridgeman Art Library 51;
Musée Condé, Chantilly/Bridgeman Art Library 55;
Phillips Auctioneers/Bridgeman Art Library 58–59.

The publisher has tried its utmost to clear copyright with
all the relevant copyright holders but if there are any additions
it will be pleased to add them.